Welcome!
Thank you for ·
I value your su·
using this Hikin

Name _____

_____

Contact _____

CONTENTS

- Welcome & A Quick Intro
- Calendars
- Hiking Bucket List
- Milestone Record
- Personal Programme (M) or (P)
- Countdown Chart
- Club Information
- Essential Kit
- Hiking Checklists
- Events Record Sheets
  +++ Over 100 Activity Pages +++
- Drawing / Blank Pages
- Review Pages

A QUICK INTRO

Circle or annotate <u>all or as many icons as you wish</u>
Use a bright shade of pen e.g. red or blue so it stands out.
Use notes section to add detail where required.
Enjoy and good luck with your Hiking!

ICON GUIDE

 (M) MAGAZINE/ GUIDE BOOK PROGRAMME

 (P) OWN PERSONAL PROGRAMME

 COUNTRYSIDE /PARK

 ROAD /URBAN ROUTE

 HILLS / RUGGED

 FOREST / REMOTE

 You can log whether you have a heavy or light loading / rucksack (User Defined)

 Specify which set of Shoes or Boots you are using. Handy when using/trying new kit
A B

 sunny
cloudy
rain
snow
windy

 TEMP
E.g.
Hot /
Mild /
Cold

My Ref ☐ Create your own Reference system for Drawings/ Camera Settings etc

THE PLAN

Walk Name **SAMPLE**

Visit No ☐
My Ref ☐

Meet up date / time/ location	Area Name National Park ☐
	Closest Town
Est. Duration	GPS / Latitude & Longitude
	Grid Ref
Est. Distance Km / Miles	Loop / Line & Back / One Way Day Trip / Overnight/ Holiday
Local Contact	Accommodation Info

THE EQUIPMENT

A B

Camera Notes

Map Name/No

THE HIKE

Start Time

End Time

Actual Distance

Total No of Steps

Calories
Burned

(M) (P)

POINTS OF INTEREST

Difficulty Level (1 Easy 5 Hard) △

Enjoyment Level (1 Bad 5 Good) ♡

Overall Grade (1 Bad 5 Good) ☆

THE EXTRAS:

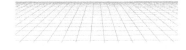

Notes
Facilities
Food & Water
Parking
Costs
Nature
Etc

100+ OF THESE ENTRY SHEETS IN THIS BOOK

Personal Best Info
Hiking Totals etc

2021

January
Su	Mo	Tu	We	Th	Fr	Sa
					1	2
3	4	5	6	7	8	9
10	11	12	13	14	15	16
17	18	19	20	21	22	23
24	25	26	27	28	29	30
31						

February
Su	Mo	Tu	We	Th	Fr	Sa
	1	2	3	4	5	6
7	8	9	10	11	12	13
14	15	16	17	18	19	20
21	22	23	24	25	26	27
28						

March
Su	Mo	Tu	We	Th	Fr	Sa
	1	2	3	4	5	6
7	8	9	10	11	12	13
14	15	16	17	18	19	20
21	22	23	24	25	26	27
28	29	30	31			

April
Su	Mo	Tu	We	Th	Fr	Sa
				1	2	3
4	5	6	7	8	9	10
11	12	13	14	15	16	17
18	19	20	21	22	23	24
25	26	27	28	29	30	

May
Su	Mo	Tu	We	Th	Fr	Sa
						1
2	3	4	5	6	7	8
9	10	11	12	13	14	15
16	17	18	19	20	21	22
23	24	25	26	27	28	29
30	31					

June
Su	Mo	Tu	We	Th	Fr	Sa
		1	2	3	4	5
6	7	8	9	10	11	12
13	14	15	16	17	18	19
20	21	22	23	24	25	26
27	28	29	30			

July
Su	Mo	Tu	We	Th	Fr	Sa
				1	2	3
4	5	6	7	8	9	10
11	12	13	14	15	16	17
18	19	20	21	22	23	24
25	26	27	28	29	30	31

August
Su	Mo	Tu	We	Th	Fr	Sa
1	2	3	4	5	6	7
8	9	10	11	12	13	14
15	16	17	18	19	20	21
22	23	24	25	26	27	28
29	30	31				

September
Su	Mo	Tu	We	Th	Fr	Sa
			1	2	3	4
5	6	7	8	9	10	11
12	13	14	15	16	17	18
19	20	21	22	23	24	25
26	27	28	29	30		

October
Su	Mo	Tu	We	Th	Fr	Sa
					1	2
3	4	5	6	7	8	9
10	11	12	13	14	15	16
17	18	19	20	21	22	23
24	25	26	27	28	29	30
31						

November
Su	Mo	Tu	We	Th	Fr	Sa
	1	2	3	4	5	6
7	8	9	10	11	12	13
14	15	16	17	18	19	20
21	22	23	24	25	26	27
28	29	30				

December
Su	Mo	Tu	We	Th	Fr	Sa
			1	2	3	4
5	6	7	8	9	10	11
12	13	14	15	16	17	18
19	20	21	22	23	24	25
26	27	28	29	30	31	

2023

January
Su	Mo	Tu	We	Th	Fr	Sa
1	2	3	4	5	6	7
8	9	10	11	12	13	14
15	16	17	18	19	20	21
22	23	24	25	26	27	28
29	30	31				

February
Su	Mo	Tu	We	Th	Fr	Sa
			1	2	3	4
5	6	7	8	9	10	11
12	13	14	15	16	17	18
19	20	21	22	23	24	25
26	27	28				

March
Su	Mo	Tu	We	Th	Fr	Sa
			1	2	3	4
5	6	7	8	9	10	11
12	13	14	15	16	17	18
19	20	21	22	23	24	25
26	27	28	29	30	31	

April
Su	Mo	Tu	We	Th	Fr	Sa
						1
2	3	4	5	6	7	8
9	10	11	12	13	14	15
16	17	18	19	20	21	22
23	24	25	26	27	28	29
30						

May
Su	Mo	Tu	We	Th	Fr	Sa
	1	2	3	4	5	6
7	8	9	10	11	12	13
14	15	16	17	18	19	20
21	22	23	24	25	26	27
28	29	30	31			

June
Su	Mo	Tu	We	Th	Fr	Sa
				1	2	3
4	5	6	7	8	9	10
11	12	13	14	15	16	17
18	19	20	21	22	23	24
25	26	27	28	29	30	

July
Su	Mo	Tu	We	Th	Fr	Sa
						1
2	3	4	5	6	7	8
9	10	11	12	13	14	15
16	17	18	19	20	21	22
23	24	25	26	27	28	29
30	31					

August
Su	Mo	Tu	We	Th	Fr	Sa
		1	2	3	4	5
6	7	8	9	10	11	12
13	14	15	16	17	18	19
20	21	22	23	24	25	26
27	28	29	30	31		

September
Su	Mo	Tu	We	Th	Fr	Sa
					1	2
3	4	5	6	7	8	9
10	11	12	13	14	15	16
17	18	19	20	21	22	23
24	25	26	27	28	29	30

October
Su	Mo	Tu	We	Th	Fr	Sa
1	2	3	4	5	6	7
8	9	10	11	12	13	14
15	16	17	18	19	20	21
22	23	24	25	26	27	28
29	30	31				

November
Su	Mo	Tu	We	Th	Fr	Sa
			1	2	3	4
5	6	7	8	9	10	11
12	13	14	15	16	17	18
19	20	21	22	23	24	25
26	27	28	29	30		

December
Su	Mo	Tu	We	Th	Fr	Sa
					1	2
3	4	5	6	7	8	9
10	11	12	13	14	15	16
17	18	19	20	21	22	23
24	25	26	27	28	29	30
31						

2022

January

Su	Mo	Tu	We	Th	Fr	Sa
						1
2	3	4	5	6	7	8
9	10	11	12	13	14	15
16	17	18	19	20	21	22
23	24	25	26	27	28	29
30	31					

February

Su	Mo	Tu	We	Th	Fr	Sa
		1	2	3	4	5
6	7	8	9	10	11	12
13	14	15	16	17	18	19
20	21	22	23	24	25	26
27	28					

March

Su	Mo	Tu	We	Th	Fr	Sa
		1	2	3	4	5
6	7	8	9	10	11	12
13	14	15	16	17	18	19
20	21	22	23	24	25	26
27	28	29	30	31		

April

Su	Mo	Tu	We	Th	Fr	Sa
					1	2
3	4	5	6	7	8	9
10	11	12	13	14	15	16
17	18	19	20	21	22	23
24	25	26	27	28	29	30

May

Su	Mo	Tu	We	Th	Fr	Sa
1	2	3	4	5	6	7
8	9	10	11	12	13	14
15	16	17	18	19	20	21
22	23	24	25	26	27	28
29	30	31				

June

Su	Mo	Tu	We	Th	Fr	Sa
			1	2	3	4
5	6	7	8	9	10	11
12	13	14	15	16	17	18
19	20	21	22	23	24	25
26	27	28	29	30		

July

Su	Mo	Tu	We	Th	Fr	Sa
					1	2
3	4	5	6	7	8	9
10	11	12	13	14	15	16
17	18	19	20	21	22	23
24	25	26	27	28	29	30
31						

August

Su	Mo	Tu	We	Th	Fr	Sa
	1	2	3	4	5	6
7	8	9	10	11	12	13
14	15	16	17	18	19	20
21	22	23	24	25	26	27
28	29	30	31			

September

Su	Mo	Tu	We	Th	Fr	Sa
				1	2	3
4	5	6	7	8	9	10
11	12	13	14	15	16	17
18	19	20	21	22	23	24
25	26	27	28	29	30	

October

Su	Mo	Tu	We	Th	Fr	Sa
						1
2	3	4	5	6	7	8
9	10	11	12	13	14	15
16	17	18	19	20	21	22
23	24	25	26	27	28	29
30	31					

November

Su	Mo	Tu	We	Th	Fr	Sa
		1	2	3	4	5
6	7	8	9	10	11	12
13	14	15	16	17	18	19
20	21	22	23	24	25	26
27	28	29	30			

December

Su	Mo	Tu	We	Th	Fr	Sa
				1	2	3
4	5	6	7	8	9	10
11	12	13	14	15	16	17
18	19	20	21	22	23	24
25	26	27	28	29	30	31

HIKING BUCKET LIST

Goals

_____
_____
_____
_____
_____
_____
_____
_____
_____

To-Do List

_____
_____
_____
_____
_____
_____
_____
_____

Notes

_____
_____
_____
_____
_____
_____
_____

"It's not the mountain we conquer, but ourselves." - Sir Edmund Hillary

NOTES

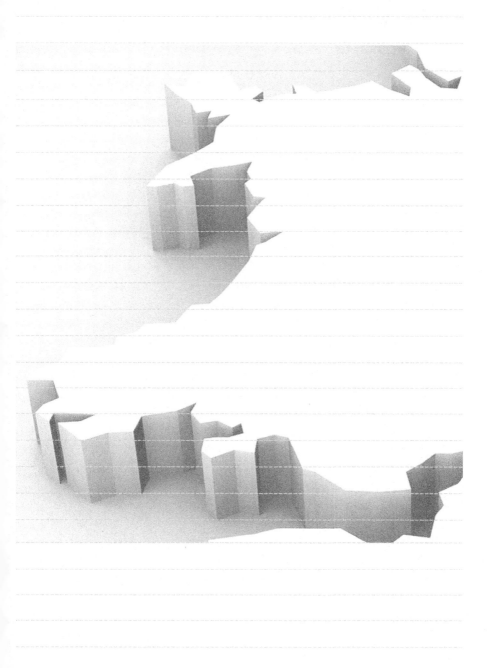

"Get going ... walk if you have to, but finish the damned race." – Ron Hill

Milestone Record

Use this to log key areas that interest you to show progression over the whole programme
E.g. Distance Covered In A Season or Number of Tors etc

Area	Date

Area	Date

Milestone Record

Use this to log key areas that interest you to show progression over the whole programme
E.g. Distance Covered In A Season or Number of Tors etc

Area	Date						

Area	Date						

PERSONAL PROGRAMME NOTES

Your hike may be part of a specific programme, for example a Magazine or Guide Book Challenge
(denoted by this symbol (M) on your record sheets)
or it may be another programme or event such as your
'Summer Holidays Challenge' where you are walking 20 trails or 100 miles etc
(denoted by (P) on the record sheets).
Use these pages to set out what your programme is. Enjoy the journey!

"There are no shortcuts to any place worth going." - Beverly Sills

"Don't fear moving slowly forward...fear standing still."
— Kathleen Harris

Countdown Chart

Use this table for example a major hike coming up or training for an event
- or just a 12 week countdown. Example headings are shown. Plan ahead. Enjoy the journey!

Weeks to go	Rest days	Suggested Distances	Actual Distances	Notes	Complete
12					
11					
10					
9					
8					
7					
6					
5					
4					
3					
2					
1					

WALKING/HIKING CLUB

Club/Group Name	
Address	
Key Contact	
Telephone Number	
Email	

Meeting Days	
Meeting Times	
Other Information	

Routes / Events / Personal Times etc

"After a day's walk, everything has twice its usual value." - G.M. Trevelyan

MY EVENTS / MEETINGS

Plan ahead. Enjoy the journey!

DATE	Event	Distance	Actual Time	Position

Notes

DATE	Event	Distance	Actual Time	Position

Notes

DATE	Event	Distance	Actual Time	Position

Notes

DATE	Event	Distance	Actual Time	Position

Notes

DATE	Event	Distance	Actual Time	Position

Notes

DATE	Event	Distance	Actual Time	Position

Notes

MY EVENTS / MEETINGS

Plan ahead. Enjoy the journey!

DATE	Event	Distance	Actual Time	Position

Notes

DATE	Event	Distance	Actual Time	Position

Notes

DATE	Event	Distance	Actual Time	Position

Notes

DATE	Event	Distance	Actual Time	Position

Notes

DATE	Event	Distance	Actual Time	Position

Notes

DATE	Event	Distance	Actual Time	Position

Notes

"When everything feels like an uphill struggle. Just think of the view from the top." - Anonymous

WALKING / HIKING PLANS

WALKING / HIKING PLAN

Event / Route   Date

1 Choose Location & Route (Check Reviews) ☐

2 Research Conditions, Weather etc ☐

3 Plan Route, Stops & Timings ☐

4 Travel Planning:How to get there & back ☐

5 Check RainFall, Sunrise & Sunset Times ☐

6 Research terrain - correct footwear ☐

7 Food & Water Requirements (refill stops etc) ☐

8 Make Equipment Packing List ☐

9 Camera Equipt, Battery solutions, Safety ☐

10 Location 'Extras': Research-
      (Points of interest,Features, Wildlife etc) ☐

ESSENTIAL KIT

This of course is dependant on the remoteness and difficulty of your hike.
But it is always useful to remind yourself and to stay safe.

1 Map & Compass, Pen Knife ☐

2 Walking Shoes / Boots & spare Dry socks ☐

3 Enough Food & Water ☐

4 (Reserve) Waterproof Clothing & Warm Hat ☐

5 First Aid Kit / Basic Repair Kit ☐

6 Sunscreen, Sun Glasses ☐

7 Fully Charged Mobile Phone / Battery Reserve ☐

8 Torch & Matches/ Lighter ☐

9 Camera Equipt, Battery solutions ☐

10 This Journal & Pen ☐

WALKING / HIKING PLAN

Event / Route   Date

1 Choose Location & Route (Check Reviews) ☐

2 Research Conditions, Weather etc ☐

3 Plan Route, Stops & Timings ☐

4 Travel Planning:How to get there & back ☐

5 Check RainFall, Sunrise & Sunset Times ☐

6 Research terrain - correct footwear ☐

7 Food & Water Requirements (refill stops etc) ☐

8 Make Equipment Packing List ☐

9 Camera Equipt, Battery solutions, Safety ☐

10 Location 'Extras': Research-
      (Points of interest,Features, Wildlife etc) ☐

ESSENTIAL KIT

This of course is dependant on the remoteness and difficulty of your hike.
But it is always useful to remind yourself and to stay safe.

1 Map & Compass, Pen Knife ☐

2 Walking Shoes / Boots & spare Dry socks ☐

3 Enough Food & Water ☐

4 (Reserve) Waterproof Clothing & Warm Hat ☐

5 First Aid Kit / Basic Repair Kit ☐

6 Sunscreen, Sun Glasses ☐

7 Fully Charged Mobile Phone / Battery Reserve ☐

8 Torch & Matches/ Lighter ☐

9 Camera Equipt, Battery solutions ☐

10 This Journal & Pen ☐

THE PLAN

Walk Name

Visit No ☐
My Ref ☐

Meet up date / time/ location

Area Name

National Park ☐

Closest Town

GPS / Latitude & Longitude

Est. Duration

Grid Ref

Est. Distance

Km
Miles

Loop / Line & Back / One Way

Day Trip / Overnight/ Holiday

Accommodation Info

Local Contact

THE EQUIPMENT

A   B

Camera Notes

Map Name/No

THE HIKE

Start Time

End Time

Actual Distance

M   P

Total No of Steps

Calories
Burned

POINTS OF INTEREST

Difficulty Level (1 Easy 5 Hard) △

Enjoyment Level (1 Bad 5 Good) ♡

Overall Grade (1 Bad 5 Good) ☆

THE EXTRAS:

Notes
Facilities
Food & Water
Parking
Costs
Nature
Etc

Personal Best Info
Hiking Totals etc

THE PLAN

Walk Name

Visit No ☐
My Ref ☐

Meet up date / time/ location

Area Name   National Park ☐

Closest Town

GPS / Latitude & Longitude

Est. Duration

Grid Ref

Est. Distance   Km / Miles

Loop / Line & Back / One Way   Day Trip / Overnight/ Holiday

Accommodation Info

Local Contact

THE EQUIPMENT

A   B

Camera Notes   Map Name/No

THE HIKE

Start Time

End Time

Actual Distance

(M) (P)

Total No of Steps   Calories Burned

POINTS OF INTEREST

Difficulty Level (1 Easy 5 Hard) △

Enjoyment Level (1 Bad 5 Good) ♡

Overall Grade (1 Bad 5 Good) ☆

THE EXTRAS:

Notes
Facilities
Food & Water
Parking
Costs
Nature
Etc

∑ Personal Best Info
Hiking Totals etc

THE PLAN

Walk Name

Visit No ☐
My Ref ☐

Meet up date / time/ location

Area Name   National Park ☐

Closest Town

Est. Duration

GPS / Latitude & Longitude

Grid Ref

Est. Distance   Km
                       Miles

Loop / Line & Back / One Way   Day Trip / Overnight/ Holiday

Accommodation Info

Local Contact

THE EQUIPMENT

A   B

Camera Notes   Map Name/No

THE HIKE

Start Time

End Time

Actual Distance

(M)   (P)

Total No of Steps   Calories
                                          Burned

POINTS OF INTEREST

Difficulty Level (1 Easy 5 Hard)   △

Enjoyment Level (1 Bad 5 Good)   ♡

Overall Grade (1 Bad 5 Good)   ☆

THE EXTRAS:

Notes
Facilities
Food & Water
Parking
Costs
Nature
Etc

Personal Best Info
Hiking Totals etc

THE PLAN

Walk Name

Visit No ☐
My Ref ☐

Meet up date / time/ location

Area Name   National Park ☐

Closest Town

GPS / Latitude & Longitude

Est. Duration

Grid Ref

Est. Distance   Km
                       Miles

Loop / Line & Back / One Way   Day Trip / Overnight/ Holiday

Accommodation Info

Local Contact

THE EQUIPMENT

A   B

Camera Notes   Map Name/No

THE HIKE

Start Time

End Time

Actual Distance

(M) (P)

Total No of Steps   Calories
                                            Burned

POINTS OF INTEREST

Difficulty Level (1 Easy 5 Hard) △

Enjoyment Level (1 Bad 5 Good) ♡

Overall Grade (1 Bad 5 Good) ☆

THE EXTRAS:

Notes
Facilities
Food & Water
Parking
Costs
Nature
Etc

Personal Best Info
Hiking Totals etc

THE PLAN

Walk Name

Visit No ☐
My Ref ☐

| Meet up date / time/ location | Area Name | National Park ☐ |

Closest Town

Est. Duration

GPS / Latitude & Longitude

Grid Ref

Est. Distance — Km / Miles

Loop / Line & Back / One Way   Day Trip / Overnight/ Holiday

Accommodation Info

Local Contact

THE EQUIPMENT

A B

Camera Notes

Map Name/No

THE HIKE

Start Time

End Time

Actual Distance

(M) (P)

Total No of Steps

Calories Burned

POINTS OF INTEREST

Difficulty Level (1 Easy 5 Hard) △

Enjoyment Level (1 Bad 5 Good) ♡

Overall Grade (1 Bad 5 Good) ☆

THE EXTRAS:

Notes
Facilities
Food & Water
Parking
Costs
Nature
Etc

Personal Best Info
Hiking Totals etc

THE PLAN

Walk Name

Visit No ☐
My Ref ☐

Meet up date / time/ location

Area Name   National Park ☐

Closest Town

GPS / Latitude & Longitude

Est. Duration

Grid Ref

Est. Distance   Km   Loop / Line & Back / One Way   Day Trip / Overnight/ Holiday
                             Miles

Accommodation Info

Local Contact

THE EQUIPMENT

A   B

Camera Notes   Map Name/No

THE HIKE

Start Time

End Time

Actual Distance

M   P

Total No of Steps   Calories
                                                     Burned

POINTS OF INTEREST

Difficulty Level (1 Easy 5 Hard) △

Enjoyment Level (1 Bad 5 Good) ♡

Overall Grade (1 Bad 5 Good) ☆

THE EXTRAS:

Notes
Facilities
Food & Water
Parking
Costs
Nature
Etc

Personal Best Info
Hiking Totals etc

THE PLAN

Walk Name

Visit No ☐
My Ref ☐

Meet up date / time/ location

Area Name
National Park ☐

Closest Town

GPS / Latitude & Longitude

Est. Duration

Grid Ref

Est. Distance _____ Km Miles

Loop / Line & Back / One Way   Day Trip / Overnight/ Holiday

Accommodation Info

Local Contact

THE EQUIPMENT

A B

Camera Notes

Map Name/No

THE HIKE

Start Time

End Time

Actual Distance

Ⓜ Ⓟ

Total No of Steps

Calories Burned

POINTS OF INTEREST

Difficulty Level (1 Easy 5 Hard) △

Enjoyment Level (1 Bad 5 Good) ♡

Overall Grade (1 Bad 5 Good) ☆

THE EXTRAS:

Notes
Facilities
Food & Water
Parking
Costs
Nature
Etc

Personal Best Info
Hiking Totals etc

THE PLAN

Walk Name

Visit No ☐
My Ref ☐

Meet up date / time/ location

Area Name

National Park ☐

Closest Town

GPS / Latitude & Longitude

Est. Duration

Grid Ref

Est. Distance   Km / Miles

Loop / Line & Back / One Way   Day Trip / Overnight/ Holiday

Accommodation Info

Local Contact

THE EQUIPMENT

A   B

Camera Notes

Map Name/No

THE HIKE

Start Time

End Time

Actual Distance

M   P

Total No of Steps   Calories Burned

POINTS OF INTEREST

Difficulty Level (1 Easy 5 Hard) △

Enjoyment Level (1 Bad 5 Good) ♡

Overall Grade (1 Bad 5 Good) ☆

THE EXTRAS:

Notes
Facilities
Food & Water
Parking
Costs
Nature
Etc

∑ Personal Best Info
Hiking Totals etc

THE PLAN

Walk Name

Visit No ☐
My Ref ☐

| Meet up date / time/ location | Area Name | National Park ☐ |

Closest Town

GPS / Latitude & Longitude

Est. Duration

Grid Ref

Est. Distance   Km
                       Miles

Loop / Line & Back / One Way   Day Trip / Overnight/ Holiday

Accommodation Info

Local Contact

THE EQUIPMENT

A   B

Camera Notes

Map Name/No

THE HIKE

Start Time

End Time

Actual Distance

(M) (P)

Total No of Steps

Calories
Burned

POINTS OF INTEREST

Difficulty Level (1 Easy 5 Hard) △

Enjoyment Level (1 Bad 5 Good) ♡

Overall Grade (1 Bad 5 Good) ☆

THE EXTRAS:

Notes
Facilities
Food & Water
Parking
Costs
Nature
Etc

Σ Personal Best Info
  Hiking Totals etc

THE PLAN

Walk Name

Visit No ☐
My Ref ☐

Meet up date / time/ location

Area Name

National Park ☐

Closest Town

GPS / Latitude & Longitude

Est. Duration

Grid Ref

Est. Distance   Km   Loop / Line & Back / One Way   Day Trip / Overnight/ Holiday
                       Miles

Accommodation Info

Local Contact

THE EQUIPMENT

A   B

Camera Notes

Map Name/No

THE HIKE

Start Time

End Time

Actual Distance

(M) (P)

Total No of Steps

Calories
Burned

POINTS OF INTEREST

Difficulty Level (1 Easy 5 Hard)   △

Enjoyment Level (1 Bad 5 Good)   ♡

Overall Grade (1 Bad 5 Good)   ☆

THE EXTRAS:

Notes
Facilities
Food & Water
Parking
Costs
Nature
Etc

Personal Best Info
Hiking Totals etc

THE PLAN

Walk Name

Visit No ☐
My Ref ☐

Meet up date / time/ location

Area Name
National Park ☐

Closest Town

Est. Duration

GPS / Latitude & Longitude

Grid Ref

Est. Distance
Km
Miles

Loop / Line & Back / One Way   Day Trip / Overnight/ Holiday

Accommodation Info

Local Contact

THE EQUIPMENT

A   B

Camera Notes

Map Name/No

THE HIKE

Start Time

End Time

Actual Distance

M   P

Total No of Steps

Calories
Burned

POINTS OF INTEREST

Difficulty Level (1 Easy 5 Hard)   △

Enjoyment Level (1 Bad 5 Good)   ♡

Overall Grade (1 Bad 5 Good)   ☆

THE EXTRAS:

Notes
Facilities
Food & Water
Parking
Costs
Nature
Etc

Personal Best Info
Hiking Totals etc

THE PLAN

Walk Name

Visit No ☐
My Ref ☐

Meet up date / time/ location

Area Name   National Park ☐

Closest Town

GPS / Latitude & Longitude

Est. Duration

Grid Ref

Est. Distance   Km   Loop / Line & Back / One Way   Day Trip / Overnight/ Holiday
                       Miles

Accommodation Info

Local Contact

THE EQUIPMENT

A B

Camera Notes   Map Name/No

THE HIKE

Start Time

End Time

Actual Distance

(M) (P)

Total No of Steps

Calories
Burned

POINTS OF INTEREST

Difficulty Level (1 Easy 5 Hard) △

Enjoyment Level (1 Bad 5 Good) ♡

Overall Grade (1 Bad 5 Good) ☆

THE EXTRAS:

Notes
Facilities
Food & Water
Parking
Costs
Nature
Etc

Personal Best Info
Hiking Totals etc

THE PLAN

Walk Name

Visit No ☐
My Ref ☐

Meet up date / time/ location

Area Name   National Park ☐

Closest Town

GPS / Latitude & Longitude

Est. Duration

Grid Ref

Est. Distance   Km
                        Miles

Loop / Line & Back / One Way   Day Trip / Overnight/ Holiday

Accommodation Info

Local Contact

THE EQUIPMENT

A   B

Camera Notes   Map Name/No

THE HIKE

Start Time

End Time

Actual Distance

Total No of Steps   Calories
                                       Burned

M   P

POINTS OF INTEREST

Difficulty Level (1 Easy 5 Hard)   △

Enjoyment Level (1 Bad 5 Good)   ♡

Overall Grade (1 Bad 5 Good)   ☆

THE EXTRAS:

Notes
Facilities
Food & Water
Parking
Costs
Nature
Etc

Σ Personal Best Info
  Hiking Totals etc

THE PLAN

Walk Name

Visit No ☐
My Ref ☐

Meet up date / time/ location

Area Name   National Park ☐

Closest Town

Est. Duration

GPS / Latitude & Longitude

Grid Ref

Est. Distance   Km Miles

Loop / Line & Back / One Way   Day Trip / Overnight/ Holiday

Accommodation Info

Local Contact

THE EQUIPMENT

A   B

Camera Notes

Map Name/No

THE HIKE

M   P

Start Time

End Time

Actual Distance

Total No of Steps

Calories Burned

POINTS OF INTEREST

Difficulty Level (1 Easy 5 Hard) △

Enjoyment Level (1 Bad 5 Good) ♡

Overall Grade (1 Bad 5 Good) ☆

THE EXTRAS:

Notes
Facilities
Food & Water
Parking
Costs
Nature
Etc

Personal Best Info
Hiking Totals etc

THE PLAN

Walk Name

Visit No ☐
My Ref ☐

Area Name   National Park ☐

Closest Town

GPS / Latitude & Longitude

Meet up date / time/ location

Grid Ref

Est. Duration

Est. Distance   Km
                       Miles

Loop / Line & Back / One Way   Day Trip / Overnight/ Holiday

Accommodation Info

Local Contact

THE EQUIPMENT

A   B

Camera Notes   Map Name/No

THE HIKE

Start Time

End Time

Actual Distance

(M) (P)

Total No of Steps   Calories
                                          Burned

POINTS OF INTEREST

Difficulty Level (1 Easy 5 Hard) △

Enjoyment Level (1 Bad 5 Good) ♡

Overall Grade (1 Bad 5 Good) ☆

THE EXTRAS:

Notes
Facilities
Food & Water
Parking
Costs
Nature
Etc

Personal Best Info
Hiking Totals etc

THE PLAN

Walk Name

Visit No ☐
My Ref ☐

Meet up date / time/ location

Area Name

National Park ☐

Closest Town

GPS / Latitude & Longitude

Est. Duration

Grid Ref

Est. Distance — Km Miles

Loop / Line & Back / One Way   Day Trip / Overnight/ Holiday

Accommodation Info

Local Contact

THE EQUIPMENT

A   B

Camera Notes

Map Name/No

THE HIKE

Start Time

End Time

Actual Distance

(M) (P)

Total No of Steps

Calories Burned

POINTS OF INTEREST

Difficulty Level (1 Easy 5 Hard)   △

Enjoyment Level (1 Bad 5 Good)   ♡

Overall Grade (1 Bad 5 Good)   ☆

THE EXTRAS:

Notes
Facilities
Food & Water
Parking
Costs
Nature
Etc

Personal Best Info
Hiking Totals etc

THE PLAN

Walk Name

Meet up date / time/ location	Area Name	National Park ☐
	Closest Town	
Est. Duration	GPS / Latitude & Longitude	
	Grid Ref	
Est. Distance Km Miles	Loop / Line & Back / One Way	Day Trip / Overnight/ Holiday
	Accommodation Info	
Local Contact		

THE EQUIPMENT

A   B

Camera Notes

Map Name/No

THE HIKE

Start Time

End Time

Actual Distance

M   P

Total No of Steps

Calories Burned

POINTS OF INTEREST

Difficulty Level (1 Easy 5 Hard) △

Enjoyment Level (1 Bad 5 Good) ♡

Overall Grade (1 Bad 5 Good) ☆

THE EXTRAS:

Notes
Facilities
Food & Water
Parking
Costs
Nature
Etc

∑ Personal Best Info
Hiking Totals etc

THE PLAN

Walk Name

Visit No ☐
My Ref ☐

Meet up date / time/ location

Area Name   National Park ☐

Closest Town

GPS / Latitude & Longitude

Est. Duration

Grid Ref

Est. Distance   Km
                        Miles

Loop / Line & Back / One Way   Day Trip / Overnight/ Holiday

Accommodation Info

Local Contact

THE EQUIPMENT

A   B

Camera Notes   Map Name/No

THE HIKE

Start Time

End Time

Actual Distance

M   P

Total No of Steps   Calories
                            Burned

POINTS OF INTEREST

Difficulty Level (1 Easy 5 Hard) △

Enjoyment Level (1 Bad 5 Good) ♡

Overall Grade (1 Bad 5 Good) ☆

THE EXTRAS:

Notes
Facilities
Food & Water
Parking
Costs
Nature
Etc

Personal Best Info
Hiking Totals etc

THE PLAN

Walk Name

Visit No ☐
My Ref ☐

Meet up date / time/ location	Area Name National Park ☐
	Closest Town
	GPS / Latitude & Longitude
Est. Duration	Grid Ref
Est. Distance Km Miles	Loop / Line & Back / One Way Day Trip / Overnight/ Holiday
Local Contact	Accommodation Info

THE EQUIPMENT

A B

Camera Notes

Map Name/No

THE HIKE

Start Time

End Time

Actual Distance

(M) (P)

Total No of Steps

Calories Burned

POINTS OF INTEREST

Difficulty Level (1 Easy 5 Hard) △

Enjoyment Level (1 Bad 5 Good) ♡

Overall Grade (1 Bad 5 Good) ☆

THE EXTRAS:

Notes
Facilities
Food & Water
Parking
Costs
Nature
Etc

Personal Best Info
Hiking Totals etc

THE PLAN

Route Name

Visit No ☐
My Ref ☐

Meet up date / time/ location

Area Name

National Park ☐

Closest Town

GPS / Latitude & Longitude

Est. Duration

Grid Ref

Est. Distance   Km Miles

Loop / Line & Back / One Way   Day Trip / Overnight / Holiday

Local Contact

Accommodation Info

THE EQUIPMENT

A   B

Camera Notes

Map Name / Ref

THE HIKE

Start Time

End Time

Actual Distance

Total No of Steps

Calories Burned

M   P

POINTS OF INTEREST

Difficulty Level (1 Easy 5 Hard) △

Enjoyment Level (1 Bad 5 Good) ♡

Overall Grade (1 Bad 5 Good) ☆

THE EXTRAS:

Notes
Facilities
Food & Water
Parking
Costs
Nature
Etc

Personal Best Info
Hiking Totals etc

THE PLAN

Route Name

Meet up date / time/ location

Area Name   National Park ☐

Closest Town

Est. Duration

GPS / Latitude & Longitude

Grid Ref

Est. Distance   Km / Miles

Loop / Line & Back / One Way   Day Trip / Overnight / Holiday

Local Contact

Accommodation Info

THE EQUIPMENT

A   B

Camera Notes   Map Name / Ref

THE HIKE

Start Time

End Time

Actual Distance

(M)   (P)

Total No of Steps   Calories Burned

POINTS OF INTEREST

Difficulty Level (1 Easy 5 Hard)   △

Enjoyment Level (1 Bad 5 Good)   ♡

Overall Grade (1 Bad 5 Good)   ☆

THE EXTRAS:

Notes
Facilities
Food & Water
Parking
Costs
Nature
Etc

∑ Personal Best Info
Hiking Totals etc

THE PLAN

Route Name

Visit No [ ]
My Ref [ ]

| Meet up date / time/ location | Area Name | National Park [ ] |
| | Closest Town | |

Est. Duration

GPS / Latitude & Longitude

Grid Ref

Est. Distance   Km / Miles   Loop / Line & Back / One Way   Day Trip / Overnight / Holiday

Accommodation Info

Local Contact

THE EQUIPMENT

A   B

Camera Notes

Map Name / Ref

THE HIKE

Start Time

End Time

Actual Distance

(M) (P)

Total No of Steps

Calories Burned

POINTS OF INTEREST

Difficulty Level (1 Easy 5 Hard) △

Enjoyment Level (1 Bad 5 Good) ♡

Overall Grade (1 Bad 5 Good) ☆

THE EXTRAS:

Notes
Facilities
Food & Water
Parking
Costs
Nature
Etc

∑ Personal Best Info
Hiking Totals etc

THE PLAN

Route Name

Visit No ☐
My Ref ☐

Meet up date / time/ location

Area Name National Park ☐

Closest Town

GPS / Latitude & Longitude

Est. Duration

Grid Ref

Est. Distance Km Miles

Loop / Line & Back / One Way   Day Trip / Overnight / Holiday

Local Contact

Accommodation Info

THE EQUIPMENT

A B

Camera Notes

Map Name / Ref

THE HIKE

Start Time

End Time

Actual Distance

M P

Total No of Steps

Calories Burned

POINTS OF INTEREST

Difficulty Level (1 Easy 5 Hard) △

Enjoyment Level (1 Bad 5 Good) ♡

Overall Grade (1 Bad 5 Good) ☆

THE EXTRAS:

Notes
Facilities
Food & Water
Parking
Costs
Nature
Etc

∑ Personal Best Info
Hiking Totals etc

THE PLAN

Route Name

Visit No ☐
My Ref ☐

Meet up date / time/ location

Area Name

National Park ☐

Closest Town

Est. Duration

GPS / Latitude & Longitude

Grid Ref

Est. Distance   Km
                       Miles

Loop / Line & Back / One Way   Day Trip / Overnight / Holiday

Accommodation Info

Local Contact

THE EQUIPMENT

A   B

Camera Notes

Map Name / Ref

THE HIKE

Start Time

End Time

Actual Distance

Total No of Steps

Calories
Burned

M   P

POINTS OF INTEREST

Difficulty Level (1 Easy 5 Hard)   △

Enjoyment Level (1 Bad 5 Good)   ♡

Overall Grade (1 Bad 5 Good)   ☆

THE EXTRAS:

Notes
Facilities
Food & Water
Parking
Costs
Nature
Etc

∑ Personal Best Info
  Hiking Totals etc

THE PLAN

Route Name

Visit No ☐

My Ref ☐

Meet up date / time/ location

Area Name

National Park ☐

Closest Town

GPS / Latitude & Longitude

Est. Duration

Grid Ref

Est. Distance   Km Miles

Loop / Line & Back / One Way

Day Trip / Overnight / Holiday

Accommodation Info

Local Contact

THE EQUIPMENT

A   B

Camera Notes

Map Name / Ref

THE HIKE

Start Time

End Time

Actual Distance

M   P

Total No of Steps

Calories Burned

POINTS OF INTEREST

Difficulty Level (1 Easy 5 Hard) △

Enjoyment Level (1 Bad 5 Good) ♡

Overall Grade (1 Bad 5 Good) ☆

THE EXTRAS:

Notes
Facilities
Food & Water
Parking
Costs
Nature
Etc

Personal Best Info
Hiking Totals etc

THE PLAN

Route Name

Visit No ☐
My Ref ☐

Meet up date / time/ location

Area Name

National Park ☐

Closest Town

GPS / Latitude & Longitude

Est. Duration

Grid Ref

Est. Distance   Km
                   Miles

Loop / Line & Back / One Way   Day Trip / Overnight / Holiday

Local Contact

Accommodation Info

THE EQUIPMENT

A B

Camera Notes

Map Name / Ref

THE HIKE

Start Time

End Time

Actual Distance

Total No of Steps

Calories
Burned

(M) (P)

POINTS OF INTEREST

Difficulty Level (1 Easy 5 Hard) △

Enjoyment Level (1 Bad 5 Good) ♡

Overall Grade (1 Bad 5 Good) ☆

THE EXTRAS:

Notes
Facilities
Food & Water
Parking
Costs
Nature
Etc

∑ Personal Best Info
Hiking Totals etc

THE PLAN

Route Name

Visit No ☐
My Ref ☐

Meet up date / time/ location

Area Name

National Park ☐

Closest Town

Est. Duration

GPS / Latitude & Longitude

Grid Ref

Est. Distance   Km Miles

Loop / Line & Back / One Way   Day Trip / Overnight / Holiday

Accommodation Info

Local Contact

THE EQUIPMENT

A   B

Camera Notes

Map Name / Ref

THE HIKE

Start Time

End Time

Actual Distance

M   P

Total No of Steps

Calories Burned

POINTS OF INTEREST

Difficulty Level (1 Easy 5 Hard) △

Enjoyment Level (1 Bad 5 Good) ♡

Overall Grade (1 Bad 5 Good) ☆

THE EXTRAS:

Notes
Facilities
Food & Water
Parking
Costs
Nature
Etc

Personal Best Info
Hiking Totals etc

THE PLAN

Route Name

Visit No ☐
My Ref ☐

Meet up date / time/ location

Area Name

National Park ☐

Closest Town

GPS / Latitude & Longitude

Est. Duration

Grid Ref

Est. Distance

Km
Miles

Loop / Line & Back / One Way

Day Trip / Overnight / Holiday

Accommodation Info

Local Contact

THE EQUIPMENT

A B

Camera Notes

Map Name / Ref

THE HIKE

Start Time

End Time

Actual Distance

Total No of Steps

Calories Burned

M P

POINTS OF INTEREST

Difficulty Level (1 Easy 5 Hard) △

Enjoyment Level (1 Bad 5 Good) ♡

Overall Grade (1 Bad 5 Good) ☆

THE EXTRAS:

Notes
Facilities
Food & Water
Parking
Costs
Nature
Etc

∑ Personal Best Info
Hiking Totals etc

THE PLAN

Route Name

Visit No ☐
My Ref ☐

Meet up date / time/ location

Area Name

National Park ☐

Closest Town

GPS / Latitude & Longitude

Est. Duration

Grid Ref

Est. Distance   Km Miles

Loop / Line & Back / One Way   Day Trip / Overnight / Holiday

Local Contact

Accommodation Info

THE EQUIPMENT

A B

Camera Notes

Map Name / Ref

THE HIKE

Start Time

End Time

Actual Distance

M   P

Total No of Steps

Calories Burned

POINTS OF INTEREST

Difficulty Level (1 Easy 5 Hard) △

Enjoyment Level (1 Bad 5 Good) ♡

Overall Grade (1 Bad 5 Good) ☆

THE EXTRAS:

Notes
Facilities
Food & Water
Parking
Costs
Nature
Etc

Personal Best Info
Hiking Totals etc

THE PLAN

Route Name

Visit No ☐
My Ref ☐

Meet up date / time/ location

Area Name   National Park ☐

Closest Town

GPS / Latitude & Longitude

Est. Duration

Grid Ref

Est. Distance   Km
                       Miles

Loop / Line & Back / One Way   Day Trip / Overnight / Holiday

Accommodation Info

Local Contact

THE EQUIPMENT

A   B

Camera Notes   Map Name / Ref

THE HIKE

Start Time

End Time

Actual Distance

M   P

Total No of Steps   Calories Burned

POINTS OF INTEREST

Difficulty Level (1 Easy 5 Hard) △

Enjoyment Level (1 Bad 5 Good) ♡

Overall Grade (1 Bad 5 Good) ☆

THE EXTRAS:

Notes
Facilities
Food & Water
Parking
Costs
Nature
Etc

∑ Personal Best Info
   Hiking Totals etc

THE PLAN

Route Name

Visit No ☐
My Ref ☐

Meet up date / time/ location

Area Name   National Park ☐

Closest Town

GPS / Latitude & Longitude

Est. Duration

Grid Ref

Est. Distance   Km
                       Miles

Loop / Line & Back / One Way   Day Trip / Overnight / Holiday

Accommodation Info

Local Contact

THE EQUIPMENT

A B

Camera Notes   Map Name / Ref

THE HIKE

Start Time

End Time

Actual Distance

Total No of Steps   Calories
                                     Burned

M   P

POINTS OF INTEREST

Difficulty Level (1 Easy 5 Hard)   △

Enjoyment Level (1 Bad 5 Good)   ♡

Overall Grade (1 Bad 5 Good)   ☆

THE EXTRAS:

Notes
Facilities
Food & Water
Parking
Costs
Nature
Etc

∑ Personal Best Info
Hiking Totals etc

THE PLAN

Route Name

Visit No ☐
My Ref ☐

Meet up date / time/ location

Area Name

National Park ☐

Closest Town

Est. Duration

GPS / Latitude & Longitude

Grid Ref

Est. Distance   Km / Miles

Loop / Line & Back / One Way   Day Trip / Overnight / Holiday

Local Contact

Accommodation Info

THE EQUIPMENT

A   B

Camera Notes

Map Name / Ref

THE HIKE

Start Time

End Time

Actual Distance

Total No of Steps

Calories Burned

M   P

POINTS OF INTEREST

Difficulty Level (1 Easy 5 Hard) △

Enjoyment Level (1 Bad 5 Good) ♡

Overall Grade (1 Bad 5 Good) ☆

THE EXTRAS:

Notes
Facilities
Food & Water
Parking
Costs
Nature
Etc

Personal Best Info
Hiking Totals etc

THE PLAN

Route Name

Visit No ☐
My Ref ☐

Meet up date / time/ location

Area Name
National Park ☐

Closest Town

GPS / Latitude & Longitude

Est. Duration

Grid Ref

Est. Distance   Km / Miles

Loop / Line & Back / One Way   Day Trip / Overnight / Holiday

Accommodation Info

Local Contact

THE EQUIPMENT

A   B

Camera Notes

Map Name / Ref

THE HIKE

Start Time

End Time

Actual Distance

(M) (P)

Total No of Steps

Calories Burned

POINTS OF INTEREST

Difficulty Level (1 Easy 5 Hard) △

Enjoyment Level (1 Bad 5 Good) ♡

Overall Grade (1 Bad 5 Good) ☆

THE EXTRAS:

Notes
Facilities
Food & Water
Parking
Costs
Nature
Etc

Personal Best Info
Hiking Totals etc

THE PLAN

Route Name

Visit No ☐
My Ref ☐

Meet up date / time/ location

Area Name

National Park ☐

Closest Town

GPS / Latitude & Longitude

Est. Duration

Grid Ref

Est. Distance

Km
Miles

Loop / Line & Back / One Way

Day Trip / Overnight / Holiday

Accommodation Info

Local Contact

THE EQUIPMENT

A   B

Camera Notes

Map Name / Ref

THE HIKE

Start Time

End Time

Actual Distance

(M) (P)

Total No of Steps

Calories
Burned

POINTS OF INTEREST

Difficulty Level (1 Easy 5 Hard) △

Enjoyment Level (1 Bad 5 Good) ♡

Overall Grade (1 Bad 5 Good) ☆

THE EXTRAS:

Notes
Facilities
Food & Water
Parking
Costs
Nature
Etc

∑ Personal Best Info
Hiking Totals etc

THE PLAN

Route Name

Visit No ☐
My Ref ☐

Meet up date / time/ location

Area Name — National Park ☐

Closest Town

Est. Duration

GPS / Latitude & Longitude

Grid Ref

Est. Distance — Km / Miles

Loop / Line & Back / One Way — Day Trip / Overnight / Holiday

Accommodation Info

Local Contact

THE EQUIPMENT

A   B

Camera Notes

Map Name / Ref

THE HIKE

Start Time

End Time

Actual Distance

(M) (P)

Total No of Steps

Calories Burned

POINTS OF INTEREST

Difficulty Level (1 Easy 5 Hard) △

Enjoyment Level (1 Bad 5 Good) ♡

Overall Grade (1 Bad 5 Good) ☆

THE EXTRAS:

Notes
Facilities
Food & Water
Parking
Costs
Nature
Etc

∑ Personal Best Info
Hiking Totals etc

THE PLAN

Route Name

Visit No ☐
My Ref ☐

Meet up date / time/ location

Area Name

National Park ☐

Closest Town

Est. Duration

GPS / Latitude & Longitude

Grid Ref

Est. Distance   Km
                       Miles

Loop / Line & Back / One Way   Day Trip / Overnight / Holiday

Local Contact

Accommodation Info

THE EQUIPMENT

A   B

Camera Notes

Map Name / Ref

THE HIKE

Start Time

End Time

Actual Distance

(M) (P)

Total No of Steps

Calories
Burned

POINTS OF INTEREST

Difficulty Level (1 Easy 5 Hard) △

Enjoyment Level (1 Bad 5 Good) ♡

Overall Grade (1 Bad 5 Good) ☆

THE EXTRAS:

Notes
Facilities
Food & Water
Parking
Costs
Nature
Etc

∑ Personal Best Info
  Hiking Totals etc

THE PLAN

Route Name

Visit No ☐
My Ref ☐

Meet up date / time/ location

Area Name

National Park ☐

Closest Town

GPS / Latitude & Longitude

Est. Duration

Grid Ref

Est. Distance   Km Miles

Loop / Line & Back / One Way   Day Trip / Overnight / Holiday

Accommodation Info

Local Contact

THE EQUIPMENT

A   B

Camera Notes

Map Name / Ref

THE HIKE

Start Time

End Time

Actual Distance

Total No of Steps   Calories Burned

POINTS OF INTEREST

Difficulty Level (1 Easy 5 Hard) △

Enjoyment Level (1 Bad 5 Good) ♡

Overall Grade (1 Bad 5 Good) ☆

THE EXTRAS:

Notes
Facilities
Food & Water
Parking
Costs
Nature
Etc

∑ Personal Best Info
  Hiking Totals etc

THE PLAN

Route Name

Visit No ☐
My Ref ☐

Meet up date / time/ location

Area Name

National Park ☐

Closest Town

Est. Duration

GPS / Latitude & Longitude

Grid Ref

Est. Distance   Km
                       Miles

Loop / Line & Back / One Way   Day Trip / Overnight / Holiday

Accommodation Info

Local Contact

THE EQUIPMENT

A   B

Camera Notes

Map Name / Ref

THE HIKE

Start Time

End Time

Actual Distance

M   P

Total No of Steps

Calories
Burned

POINTS OF INTEREST

Difficulty Level (1 Easy 5 Hard) △

Enjoyment Level (1 Bad 5 Good) ♡

Overall Grade (1 Bad 5 Good) ☆

THE EXTRAS:

Notes
Facilities
Food & Water
Parking
Costs
Nature
Etc

Personal Best Info
Hiking Totals etc

THE PLAN

Route Name

Visit No ☐
My Ref ☐

Meet up date / time/ location

Area Name   National Park ☐

Closest Town

GPS / Latitude & Longitude

Est. Duration

Grid Ref

Est. Distance   Km
                                 Miles

Loop / Line & Back / One Way   Day Trip / Overnight / Holiday

Accommodation Info

Local Contact

THE EQUIPMENT

A   B

Camera Notes   Map Name / Ref

THE HIKE

Start Time

End Time

Actual Distance

(M) (P)

Total No of Steps   Calories
                                               Burned

POINTS OF INTEREST

Difficulty Level (1 Easy 5 Hard) △

Enjoyment Level (1 Bad 5 Good) ♡

Overall Grade (1 Bad 5 Good) ☆

THE EXTRAS:

Notes
Facilities
Food & Water
Parking
Costs
Nature
Etc

∑ Personal Best Info
Hiking Totals etc

THE PLAN

Route Name

Visit No ☐
My Ref ☐

Meet up date / time/ location

Area Name National Park ☐

Closest Town

GPS / Latitude & Longitude

Est. Duration

Grid Ref

Est. Distance Km Miles

Loop / Line & Back / One Way   Day Trip / Overnight / Holiday

Local Contact

Accommodation Info

THE EQUIPMENT

A B

Camera Notes

Map Name / Ref

THE HIKE

Start Time

End Time

Actual Distance

M   P

Total No of Steps

Calories Burned

POINTS OF INTEREST

Difficulty Level (1 Easy 5 Hard) △

Enjoyment Level (1 Bad 5 Good) ♡

Overall Grade (1 Bad 5 Good) ☆

THE EXTRAS:

Notes
Facilities
Food & Water
Parking
Costs
Nature
Etc

Personal Best Info
Hiking Totals etc

THE PLAN

Route Name

Visit No ☐
My Ref ☐

Meet up date / time/ location

Area Name

National Park ☐

Closest Town

GPS / Latitude & Longitude

Est. Duration

Grid Ref

Est. Distance   Km Miles

Loop / Line & Back / One Way   Day Trip / Overnight / Holiday

Accommodation Info

Local Contact

THE EQUIPMENT

A   B

Camera Notes

Map Name / Ref

THE HIKE

Start Time

End Time

Actual Distance

M   P

Total No of Steps

Calories Burned

POINTS OF INTEREST

Difficulty Level (1 Easy 5 Hard) △

Enjoyment Level (1 Bad 5 Good) ♡

Overall Grade (1 Bad 5 Good) ☆

THE EXTRAS:

Notes
Facilities
Food & Water
Parking
Costs
Nature
Etc

Personal Best Info
Hiking Totals etc

THE PLAN

Route Name

Visit No ☐
My Ref ☐

Meet up date / time/ location

Area Name   National Park ☐

Closest Town

Est. Duration

GPS / Latitude & Longitude

Grid Ref

Est. Distance   Km
                       Miles

Loop / Line & Back / One Way   Day Trip / Overnight / Holiday

Local Contact

Accommodation Info

THE EQUIPMENT

A   B

Camera Notes

Map Name / Ref

THE HIKE

Start Time

End Time

Actual Distance

(M) (P)

Total No of Steps

Calories
Burned

POINTS OF INTEREST

Difficulty Level (1 Easy 5 Hard) △

Enjoyment Level (1 Bad 5 Good) ♡

Overall Grade (1 Bad 5 Good) ☆

THE EXTRAS:

Notes
Facilities
Food & Water
Parking
Costs
Nature
Etc

∑ Personal Best Info
  Hiking Totals etc

THE PLAN

Route Name

Visit No ☐
My Ref ☐

Meet up date / time/ location

Area Name   National Park ☐

Closest Town

GPS / Latitude & Longitude

Est. Duration

Grid Ref

Est. Distance   Km / Miles

Loop / Line & Back / One Way   Day Trip / Overnight / Holiday

Accommodation Info

Local Contact

THE EQUIPMENT

A   B

Camera Notes

Map Name / Ref

THE HIKE

Start Time

End Time

Actual Distance

(M) (P)

Total No of Steps

Calories Burned

POINTS OF INTEREST

Difficulty Level (1 Easy 5 Hard) △

Enjoyment Level (1 Bad 5 Good) ♡

Overall Grade (1 Bad 5 Good) ☆

THE EXTRAS:

Notes
Facilities
Food & Water
Parking
Costs
Nature
Etc

Personal Best Info
Hiking Totals etc

THE PLAN

Route Name

Visit No ☐
My Ref ☐

Meet up date / time/ location

Area Name

National Park ☐

Closest Town

Est. Duration

GPS / Latitude & Longitude

Grid Ref

Est. Distance   Km
                    Miles

Loop / Line & Back / One Way   Day Trip / Overnight / Holiday

Accommodation Info

Local Contact

THE EQUIPMENT

A   B

Camera Notes

Map Name / Ref

THE HIKE

Start Time

End Time

Actual Distance

M   P

Total No of Steps

Calories
Burned

POINTS OF INTEREST

Difficulty Level (1 Easy 5 Hard) △

Enjoyment Level (1 Bad 5 Good) ♡

Overall Grade (1 Bad 5 Good) ☆

THE EXTRAS:

Notes
Facilities
Food & Water
Parking
Costs
Nature
Etc

∑ Personal Best Info
  Hiking Totals etc

THE PLAN

Route Name

Visit No ☐
My Ref ☐

Meet up date / time/ location

Area Name

National Park ☐

Closest Town

GPS / Latitude & Longitude

Est. Duration

Grid Ref

Est. Distance — Km / Miles

Loop / Line & Back / One Way   Day Trip / Overnight / Holiday

Accommodation Info

Local Contact

THE EQUIPMENT

A   B

Camera Notes

Map Name / Ref

THE HIKE

Start Time

End Time

Actual Distance

Total No of Steps

Calories Burned

(M) (P)

POINTS OF INTEREST

Difficulty Level (1 Easy 5 Hard) △

Enjoyment Level (1 Bad 5 Good) ♡

Overall Grade (1 Bad 5 Good) ☆

THE EXTRAS:

Notes
Facilities
Food & Water
Parking
Costs
Nature
Etc

Personal Best Info
Hiking Totals etc

THE PLAN

Route Name

Visit No [ ]
My Ref [ ]

Meet up date / time/ location

Area Name
National Park [ ]

Closest Town

GPS / Latitude & Longitude

Est. Duration

Grid Ref

Est. Distance   Km
                       Miles

Loop / Line & Back / One Way   Day Trip / Overnight / Holiday

Accommodation Info

Local Contact

THE EQUIPMENT

A   B

Camera Notes

Map Name / Ref

THE HIKE

Start Time

End Time

Actual Distance

(M) (P)

Total No of Steps

Calories
Burned

POINTS OF INTEREST

Difficulty Level (1 Easy 5 Hard)   △

Enjoyment Level (1 Bad 5 Good)   ♡

Overall Grade (1 Bad 5 Good)   ☆

THE EXTRAS:

Notes
Facilities
Food & Water
Parking
Costs
Nature
Etc

∑ Personal Best Info
Hiking Totals etc

THE PLAN

Route Name

Visit No ☐
My Ref ☐

Meet up date / time/ location

Area Name

National Park ☐

Closest Town

GPS / Latitude & Longitude

Est. Duration

Grid Ref

Est. Distance   Km
                       Miles

Loop / Line & Back / One Way   Day Trip / Overnight / Holiday

Local Contact

Accommodation Info

THE EQUIPMENT

A   B

Camera Notes

Map Name / Ref

THE HIKE

Start Time

End Time

Actual Distance

Total No of Steps

Calories Burned

(M) (P)

POINTS OF INTEREST

Difficulty Level (1 Easy 5 Hard) △

Enjoyment Level (1 Bad 5 Good) ♡

Overall Grade (1 Bad 5 Good) ☆

THE EXTRAS:

Notes
Facilities
Food & Water
Parking
Costs
Nature
Etc

∑ Personal Best Info
  Hiking Totals etc

THE PLAN

Route Name

Visit No ☐
My Ref ☐

Meet up date / time/ location

Area Name — National Park ☐

Closest Town

GPS / Latitude & Longitude

Est. Duration

Grid Ref

Est. Distance — Km / Miles

Loop / Line & Back / One Way   Day Trip / Overnight / Holiday

Accommodation Info

Local Contact

THE EQUIPMENT

A   B

Camera Notes — Map Name / Ref

THE HIKE

Start Time

End Time

Actual Distance

(M)   (P)

Total No of Steps — Calories Burned

POINTS OF INTEREST

Difficulty Level (1 Easy 5 Hard) △

Enjoyment Level (1 Bad 5 Good) ♡

Overall Grade (1 Bad 5 Good) ☆

THE EXTRAS:

Notes
Facilities
Food & Water
Parking
Costs
Nature
Etc

∑ Personal Best Info
Hiking Totals etc

THE PLAN

Route Name

Meet up date / time/ location

Area Name

National Park ☐

Closest Town

GPS / Latitude & Longitude

Est. Duration

Grid Ref

Est. Distance Km Miles

Loop / Line & Back / One Way   Day Trip / Overnight / Holiday

Accommodation Info

Local Contact

THE EQUIPMENT

A   B

Camera Notes

Map Name / Ref

THE HIKE

Start Time

End Time

Actual Distance

(M) (P)

Total No of Steps

Calories Burned

POINTS OF INTEREST

Difficulty Level (1 Easy 5 Hard) △

Enjoyment Level (1 Bad 5 Good) ♡

Overall Grade (1 Bad 5 Good) ☆

THE EXTRAS:

Notes
Facilities
Food & Water
Parking
Costs
Nature
Etc

∑ Personal Best Info
Hiking Totals etc

THE PLAN

Route Name

Visit No ☐
My Ref ☐

Meet up date / time/ location

Area Name

National Park ☐

Closest Town

Est. Duration

GPS / Latitude & Longitude

Grid Ref

Est. Distance   Km Miles

Loop / Line & Back / One Way   Day Trip / Overnight / Holiday

Local Contact

Accommodation Info

THE EQUIPMENT

A   B

Camera Notes

Map Name / Ref

THE HIKE

Start Time

End Time

Actual Distance

Ⓜ Ⓟ

Total No of Steps

Calories Burned

POINTS OF INTEREST

Difficulty Level (1 Easy 5 Hard) △

Enjoyment Level (1 Bad 5 Good) ♡

Overall Grade (1 Bad 5 Good) ☆

THE EXTRAS:

Notes
Facilities
Food & Water
Parking
Costs
Nature
Etc

∑ Personal Best Info
Hiking Totals etc

THE PLAN

Route Name

Visit No ☐
My Ref ☐

Meet up date / time/ location

Area Name

National Park ☐

Closest Town

GPS / Latitude & Longitude

Est. Duration

Grid Ref

Est. Distance

Km
Miles

Loop / Line & Back / One Way

Day Trip / Overnight / Holiday

Local Contact

Accommodation Info

THE EQUIPMENT

A   B

Camera Notes

Map Name / Ref

THE HIKE

Start Time

End Time

Actual Distance

Total No of Steps

Calories
Burned

(M)   (P)

POINTS OF INTEREST

Difficulty Level (1 Easy 5 Hard) △

Enjoyment Level (1 Bad 5 Good) ♡

Overall Grade (1 Bad 5 Good) ☆

THE EXTRAS:

Notes
Facilities
Food & Water
Parking
Costs
Nature
Etc

Σ Personal Best Info
Hiking Totals etc

THE PLAN

Route Name

Visit No ☐
My Ref ☐

Meet up date / time/ location

Area Name

National Park ☐

Closest Town

GPS / Latitude & Longitude

Est. Duration

Grid Ref

Est. Distance   Km Miles

Loop / Line & Back / One Way   Day Trip / Overnight / Holiday

Accommodation Info

Local Contact

THE EQUIPMENT

A   B

Camera Notes

Map Name / Ref

THE HIKE

Start Time

End Time

Actual Distance

(M) (P)

Total No of Steps

Calories Burned

POINTS OF INTEREST

Difficulty Level (1 Easy 5 Hard) △

Enjoyment Level (1 Bad 5 Good) ♡

Overall Grade (1 Bad 5 Good) ☆

THE EXTRAS:

Notes
Facilities
Food & Water
Parking
Costs
Nature
Etc

∑ Personal Best Info
Hiking Totals etc

THE PLAN

Route Name

Visit No ☐
My Ref ☐

Meet up date / time/ location

Area Name — National Park ☐

Closest Town

GPS / Latitude & Longitude

Est. Duration

Grid Ref

Est. Distance — Km / Miles

Loop / Line & Back / One Way — Day Trip / Overnight / Holiday

Accommodation Info

Local Contact

THE EQUIPMENT

A   B

Camera Notes

Map Name / Ref

THE HIKE

Start Time

End Time

Actual Distance

(M) (P)

Total No of Steps

Calories Burned

POINTS OF INTEREST

Difficulty Level (1 Easy 5 Hard) △

Enjoyment Level (1 Bad 5 Good) ♡

Overall Grade (1 Bad 5 Good) ☆

THE EXTRAS:

Notes
Facilities
Food & Water
Parking
Costs
Nature
Etc

∑ Personal Best Info
Hiking Totals etc

THE PLAN

Route Name

Visit No ☐
My Ref ☐

Meet up date / time/ location

Area Name

National Park ☐

Closest Town

GPS / Latitude & Longitude

Est. Duration

Grid Ref

Est. Distance   Km / Miles

Loop / Line & Back / One Way   Day Trip / Overnight / Holiday

Accommodation Info

Local Contact

THE EQUIPMENT

A   B

Camera Notes

Map Name / Ref

THE HIKE

Start Time

End Time

Actual Distance

M   P

Total No of Steps

Calories Burned

POINTS OF INTEREST

Difficulty Level (1 Easy 5 Hard) △

Enjoyment Level (1 Bad 5 Good) ♡

Overall Grade (1 Bad 5 Good) ☆

THE EXTRAS:

Notes
Facilities
Food & Water
Parking
Costs
Nature
Etc

Personal Best Info
Hiking Totals etc

THE PLAN

Route Name

Visit No ☐
My Ref ☐

Meet up date / time/ location

Area Name

National Park ☐

Closest Town

GPS / Latitude & Longitude

Est. Duration

Grid Ref

Est. Distance | Km Miles

Loop / Line & Back / One Way

Day Trip / Overnight / Holiday

Accommodation Info

Local Contact

THE EQUIPMENT

A   B

Camera Notes

Map Name / Ref

THE HIKE

Start Time

End Time

Actual Distance

M   P

Total No of Steps

Calories Burned

POINTS OF INTEREST

Difficulty Level (1 Easy 5 Hard) △

Enjoyment Level (1 Bad 5 Good) ♡

Overall Grade (1 Bad 5 Good) ☆

THE EXTRAS:

Notes
Facilities
Food & Water
Parking
Costs
Nature
Etc

∑ Personal Best Info
Hiking Totals etc

THE PLAN

Route Name

Meet up date / time/ location

Area Name   National Park ☐

Closest Town

Est. Duration

GPS / Latitude & Longitude

Grid Ref

Est. Distance   Km / Miles

Loop / Line & Back / One Way   Day Trip / Overnight / Holiday

Local Contact

Accommodation Info

THE EQUIPMENT

A   B

Camera Notes

Map Name / Ref

THE HIKE

Start Time

End Time

Actual Distance

Total No of Steps

Calories Burned

M   P

POINTS OF INTEREST

Difficulty Level (1 Easy 5 Hard) △

Enjoyment Level (1 Bad 5 Good) ♡

Overall Grade (1 Bad 5 Good) ☆

THE EXTRAS:

Notes
Facilities
Food & Water
Parking
Costs
Nature
Etc

Personal Best Info
Hiking Totals etc

THE PLAN

Route Name

Visit No ☐
My Ref ☐

Meet up date / time/ location

Area Name   National Park ☐

Closest Town

GPS / Latitude & Longitude

Est. Duration

Grid Ref

Est. Distance   Km / Miles

Loop / Line & Back / One Way   Day Trip / Overnight / Holiday

Accommodation Info

Local Contact

THE EQUIPMENT

A   B

Camera Notes   Map Name / Ref

THE HIKE

Start Time

End Time

Actual Distance

(M)   (P)

Total No of Steps   Calories Burned

POINTS OF INTEREST

Difficulty Level (1 Easy 5 Hard) △

Enjoyment Level (1 Bad 5 Good) ♡

Overall Grade (1 Bad 5 Good) ☆

THE EXTRAS:

Notes
Facilities
Food & Water
Parking
Costs
Nature
Etc

Personal Best Info
Hiking Totals etc

THE PLAN

Route Name

Visit No ☐
My Ref ☐

Meet up date / time/ location

Area Name — National Park ☐

Closest Town

GPS / Latitude & Longitude

Est. Duration

Grid Ref

Est. Distance — Km / Miles

Loop / Line & Back / One Way — Day Trip / Overnight / Holiday

Accommodation Info

Local Contact

THE EQUIPMENT

A   B

Camera Notes

Map Name / Ref

THE HIKE

Start Time

End Time

Actual Distance

M   P

Total No of Steps — Calories Burned

POINTS OF INTEREST

Difficulty Level (1 Easy 5 Hard) △

Enjoyment Level (1 Bad 5 Good) ♡

Overall Grade (1 Bad 5 Good) ☆

THE EXTRAS:

Notes
Facilities
Food & Water
Parking
Costs
Nature
Etc

∑ Personal Best Info
Hiking Totals etc

THE PLAN

Route Name

Visit No ☐
My Ref ☐

Meet up date / time/ location

Area Name　　　　　　　　National Park ☐

Closest Town

GPS / Latitude & Longitude

Est. Duration

Grid Ref

Est. Distance　　Km / Miles　　Loop / Line & Back / One Way　　Day Trip / Overnight / Holiday

Accommodation Info

Local Contact

THE EQUIPMENT

A　B

Camera Notes　　　　　　　　　　　　　　　　Map Name / Ref

THE HIKE

Start Time

End Time

Actual Distance

(M)　(P)

Total No of Steps　　　　　　Calories Burned

POINTS OF INTEREST

Difficulty Level (1 Easy 5 Hard) △

Enjoyment Level (1 Bad 5 Good) ♡

Overall Grade (1 Bad 5 Good) ☆

THE EXTRAS:

Notes
Facilities
Food & Water
Parking
Costs
Nature
Etc

Personal Best Info
Hiking Totals etc

THE PLAN

Route Name

Visit No ☐
My Ref ☐

Meet up date / time/ location

Area Name

National Park ☐

Closest Town

Est. Duration

GPS / Latitude & Longitude

Grid Ref

Est. Distance   Km
                       Miles

Loop / Line & Back / One Way   Day Trip / Overnight / Holiday

Accommodation Info

Local Contact

THE EQUIPMENT

A   B

Camera Notes

Map Name / Ref

THE HIKE

Start Time

End Time

Actual Distance

Ⓜ   Ⓟ

Total No of Steps

Calories
Burned

POINTS OF INTEREST

Difficulty Level (1 Easy 5 Hard)   △

Enjoyment Level (1 Bad 5 Good)   ♡

Overall Grade (1 Bad 5 Good)   ☆

THE EXTRAS:

Notes
Facilities
Food & Water
Parking
Costs
Nature
Etc

∑ Personal Best Info
Hiking Totals etc

THE PLAN

Route Name

Visit No ☐
My Ref ☐

Meet up date / time/ location

Area Name   National Park ☐

Closest Town

GPS / Latitude & Longitude

Est. Duration

Grid Ref

Est. Distance   Km
                        Miles

Loop / Line & Back / One Way   Day Trip / Overnight / Holiday

Accommodation Info

Local Contact

THE EQUIPMENT

A   B

Camera Notes

Map Name / Ref

THE HIKE

Start Time

End Time

Actual Distance

M   P

Total No of Steps

Calories
Burned

POINTS OF INTEREST

Difficulty Level (1 Easy 5 Hard) △

Enjoyment Level (1 Bad 5 Good) ♡

Overall Grade (1 Bad 5 Good) ☆

THE EXTRAS:

Notes
Facilities
Food & Water
Parking
Costs
Nature
Etc

Personal Best Info
Hiking Totals etc

THE PLAN

Route Name

Visit No ☐
My Ref ☐

Meet up date / time/ location

Area Name

National Park ☐

Closest Town

Est. Duration

GPS / Latitude & Longitude

Grid Ref

Est. Distance — Km Miles

Loop / Line & Back / One Way   Day Trip / Overnight / Holiday

Local Contact

Accommodation Info

THE EQUIPMENT

A   B

Camera Notes

Map Name / Ref

THE HIKE

Start Time

End Time

Actual Distance

(M) (P)

Total No of Steps

Calories Burned

POINTS OF INTEREST

Difficulty Level (1 Easy 5 Hard) △

Enjoyment Level (1 Bad 5 Good) ♡

Overall Grade (1 Bad 5 Good) ☆

THE EXTRAS:

Notes
Facilities
Food & Water
Parking
Costs
Nature
Etc

∑ Personal Best Info
Hiking Totals etc

THE PLAN

Route Name

Visit No ☐
My Ref ☐

Meet up date / time/ location

Area Name   National Park ☐

Closest Town

GPS / Latitude & Longitude

Est. Duration

Grid Ref

Est. Distance   Km
                       Miles

Loop / Line & Back / One Way   Day Trip / Overnight / Holiday

Accommodation Info

Local Contact

THE EQUIPMENT

A   B

Camera Notes   Map Name / Ref

THE HIKE

Start Time

End Time

Actual Distance

(M) (P)

Total No of Steps   Calories Burned

POINTS OF INTEREST

Difficulty Level (1 Easy 5 Hard) △

Enjoyment Level (1 Bad 5 Good) ♡

Overall Grade (1 Bad 5 Good) ☆

THE EXTRAS:

Notes
Facilities
Food & Water
Parking
Costs
Nature
Etc

Personal Best Info
Hiking Totals etc

THE PLAN

Route Name

Visit No ☐
My Ref ☐

Meet up date / time/ location

Area Name
National Park ☐

Closest Town

Est. Duration

GPS / Latitude & Longitude

Est. Distance   Km Miles

Grid Ref

Loop / Line & Back / One Way   Day Trip / Overnight / Holiday

Local Contact

Accommodation Info

THE EQUIPMENT

A   B

Camera Notes

Map Name / Ref

THE HIKE

Start Time

End Time

Actual Distance

(M) (P)

Total No of Steps

Calories Burned

POINTS OF INTEREST

Difficulty Level (1 Easy 5 Hard) △

Enjoyment Level (1 Bad 5 Good) ♡

Overall Grade (1 Bad 5 Good) ☆

THE EXTRAS:

Notes
Facilities
Food & Water
Parking
Costs
Nature
Etc

∑ Personal Best Info
Hiking Totals etc

THE PLAN

Route Name

Visit No

My Ref

Meet up date / time/ location

Area Name

National Park

Closest Town

GPS / Latitude & Longitude

Est. Duration

Grid Ref

Est. Distance

Km
Miles

Loop / Line & Back / One Way

Day Trip / Overnight / Holiday

Accommodation Info

Local Contact

THE EQUIPMENT

A   B

Camera Notes

Map Name / Ref

THE HIKE

Start Time

End Time

Actual Distance

Total No of Steps

Calories Burned

M   P

POINTS OF INTEREST

Difficulty Level (1 Easy 5 Hard)

Enjoyment Level (1 Bad 5 Good)

Overall Grade (1 Bad 5 Good)

THE EXTRAS:

Notes
Facilities
Food & Water
Parking
Costs
Nature
Etc

∑ Personal Best Info
Hiking Totals etc

THE PLAN

Route Name

Visit No ☐
My Ref ☐

Meet up date / time/ location

Area Name   National Park ☐

Closest Town

GPS / Latitude & Longitude

Est. Duration

Grid Ref

Est. Distance   Km / Miles

Loop / Line & Back / One Way   Day Trip / Overnight / Holiday

Accommodation Info

Local Contact

THE EQUIPMENT

A   B

Camera Notes

Map Name / Ref

THE HIKE

Start Time

End Time

Actual Distance

Total No of Steps   Calories Burned

Ⓜ Ⓟ

POINTS OF INTEREST

Difficulty Level (1 Easy 5 Hard) △

Enjoyment Level (1 Bad 5 Good) ♡

Overall Grade (1 Bad 5 Good) ☆

THE EXTRAS:

Notes
Facilities
Food & Water
Parking
Costs
Nature
Etc

∑ Personal Best Info
Hiking Totals etc

THE PLAN

Route Name

Visit No ☐
My Ref ☐

Meet up date / time/ location

Area Name

National Park ☐

Closest Town

Est. Duration

GPS / Latitude & Longitude

Grid Ref

Est. Distance   Km / Miles

Loop / Line & Back / One Way   Day Trip / Overnight / Holiday

Accommodation Info

Local Contact

THE EQUIPMENT

A B

Camera Notes

Map Name / Ref

THE HIKE

Start Time

End Time

Actual Distance

Total No of Steps

Calories Burned

M P

POINTS OF INTEREST

Difficulty Level (1 Easy 5 Hard) △

Enjoyment Level (1 Bad 5 Good) ♡

Overall Grade (1 Bad 5 Good) ☆

THE EXTRAS:

Notes
Facilities
Food & Water
Parking
Costs
Nature
Etc

Personal Best Info
Hiking Totals etc

THE PLAN

Route Name

Visit No ☐
My Ref ☐

Meet up date / time/ location

Area Name   National Park ☐

Closest Town

GPS / Latitude & Longitude

Est. Duration

Grid Ref

Est. Distance   Km / Miles   Loop / Line & Back / One Way   Day Trip / Overnight / Holiday

Accommodation Info

Local Contact

THE EQUIPMENT

A   B

Camera Notes   Map Name / Ref

THE HIKE

Start Time

End Time

Actual Distance

(M) (P)

Total No of Steps   Calories Burned

POINTS OF INTEREST

Difficulty Level (1 Easy 5 Hard) △

Enjoyment Level (1 Bad 5 Good) ♡

Overall Grade (1 Bad 5 Good) ☆

THE EXTRAS:

Notes
Facilities
Food & Water
Parking
Costs
Nature
Etc

Σ Personal Best Info
  Hiking Totals etc

THE PLAN

Route Name

Visit No ☐
My Ref ☐

Meet up date / time/ location	Area Name National Park ☐
	Closest Town
Est. Duration	GPS / Latitude & Longitude
	Grid Ref
Est. Distance Km / Miles	Loop / Line & Back / One Way Day Trip / Overnight / Holiday
Local Contact	Accommodation Info

THE EQUIPMENT

A   B

Camera Notes

Map Name / Ref

THE HIKE

Start Time

End Time

Actual Distance

M   P

Total No of Steps   Calories Burned

POINTS OF INTEREST

Difficulty Level (1 Easy 5 Hard) △

Enjoyment Level (1 Bad 5 Good) ♡

Overall Grade (1 Bad 5 Good) ☆

THE EXTRAS:

Notes
Facilities
Food & Water
Parking
Costs
Nature
Etc

Personal Best Info
Hiking Totals etc

THE PLAN

Route Name

Visit No ☐
My Ref ☐

Meet up date / time/ location

Area Name   National Park ☐

Closest Town

GPS / Latitude & Longitude

Est. Duration

Grid Ref

Est. Distance   Km   Loop / Line & Back / One Way   Day Trip / Overnight / Holiday
                       Miles

Accommodation Info

Local Contact

THE EQUIPMENT

A   B

Camera Notes   Map Name / Ref

THE HIKE

Start Time

End Time

Actual Distance

M   P

Total No of Steps   Calories
                                     Burned

POINTS OF INTEREST

Difficulty Level (1 Easy 5 Hard) △

Enjoyment Level (1 Bad 5 Good) ♡

Overall Grade (1 Bad 5 Good) ☆

THE EXTRAS:

Notes
Facilities
Food & Water
Parking
Costs
Nature
Etc

∑ Personal Best Info
  Hiking Totals etc

THE PLAN

Route Name

Visit No ☐
My Ref ☐

Meet up date / time/ location

Area Name   National Park ☐

Closest Town

GPS / Latitude & Longitude

Est. Duration

Grid Ref

Est. Distance   Km
                        Miles

Loop / Line & Back / One Way   Day Trip / Overnight / Holiday

Accommodation Info

Local Contact

THE EQUIPMENT

A   B

Camera Notes   Map Name / Ref

THE HIKE

Start Time

End Time

Actual Distance

M   P

Total No of Steps   Calories
                                             Burned

POINTS OF INTEREST

Difficulty Level (1 Easy 5 Hard)   △

Enjoyment Level (1 Bad 5 Good)   ♡

Overall Grade (1 Bad 5 Good)   ☆

THE EXTRAS:

Notes
Facilities
Food & Water
Parking
Costs
Nature
Etc

Personal Best Info
Hiking Totals etc

THE PLAN

Route Name

Visit No ☐
My Ref ☐

Meet up date / time/ location

Area Name

National Park ☐

Closest Town

GPS / Latitude & Longitude

Est. Duration

Grid Ref

Est. Distance — Km / Miles

Loop / Line & Back / One Way   Day Trip / Overnight / Holiday

Accommodation Info

Local Contact

THE EQUIPMENT

A   B

Camera Notes

Map Name / Ref

THE HIKE

Start Time

End Time

Actual Distance

M   P

Total No of Steps

Calories Burned

POINTS OF INTEREST

Difficulty Level (1 Easy 5 Hard) △

Enjoyment Level (1 Bad 5 Good) ♡

Overall Grade (1 Bad 5 Good) ☆

THE EXTRAS:

Notes
Facilities
Food & Water
Parking
Costs
Nature
Etc

Personal Best Info
Hiking Totals etc

THE PLAN

Route Name

Meet up date / time/ location

Area Name   National Park ☐

Closest Town

GPS / Latitude & Longitude

Est. Duration

Grid Ref

Est. Distance   Km / Miles   Loop / Line & Back / One Way   Day Trip / Overnight / Holiday

Accommodation Info

Local Contact

THE EQUIPMENT

A   B

Camera Notes   Map Name / Ref

THE HIKE

Start Time

End Time

Actual Distance

M   P

Total No of Steps   Calories Burned

POINTS OF INTEREST

Difficulty Level (1 Easy 5 Hard) △

Enjoyment Level (1 Bad 5 Good) ♡

Overall Grade (1 Bad 5 Good) ☆

THE EXTRAS:

Notes
Facilities
Food & Water
Parking
Costs
Nature
Etc

∑ Personal Best Info
Hiking Totals etc

THE PLAN

Route Name

Visit No ☐

My Ref ☐

Meet up date / time/ location

Area Name National Park ☐

Closest Town

GPS / Latitude & Longitude

Est. Duration

Grid Ref

Est. Distance Km / Miles Loop / Line & Back / One Way   Day Trip / Overnight / Holiday

Accommodation Info

Local Contact

THE EQUIPMENT

A B

Camera Notes

Map Name / Ref

THE HIKE

Start Time

End Time

Actual Distance

M P

Total No of Steps

Calories Burned

POINTS OF INTEREST

Difficulty Level (1 Easy 5 Hard) △

Enjoyment Level (1 Bad 5 Good) ♡

Overall Grade (1 Bad 5 Good) ☆

THE EXTRAS:

Notes
Facilities
Food & Water
Parking
Costs
Nature
Etc

Personal Best Info
Hiking Totals etc

THE PLAN

Route Name

Visit No ☐
My Ref ☐

Meet up date / time/ location

Area Name
National Park ☐

Closest Town

Est. Duration

GPS / Latitude & Longitude

Grid Ref

Est. Distance
Km
Miles

Loop / Line & Back / One Way   Day Trip / Overnight / Holiday

Accommodation Info

Local Contact

THE EQUIPMENT

A   B

Camera Notes

Map Name / Ref

THE HIKE

Start Time

End Time

Actual Distance

(M) (P)

Total No of Steps

Calories Burned

POINTS OF INTEREST

Difficulty Level (1 Easy 5 Hard) △

Enjoyment Level (1 Bad 5 Good) ♡

Overall Grade (1 Bad 5 Good) ☆

THE EXTRAS:

Notes
Facilities
Food & Water
Parking
Costs
Nature
Etc

Personal Best Info
Hiking Totals etc

THE PLAN

Route Name

Visit No ☐
My Ref ☐

Meet up date / time/ location

Area Name   National Park ☐

Closest Town

GPS / Latitude & Longitude

Est. Duration

Grid Ref

Est. Distance   Km / Miles

Loop / Line & Back / One Way   Day Trip / Overnight / Holiday

Accommodation Info

Local Contact

THE EQUIPMENT

A   B

Camera Notes

Map Name / Ref

THE HIKE

Start Time

End Time

Actual Distance

(M) (P)

Total No of Steps   Calories Burned

POINTS OF INTEREST

Difficulty Level (1 Easy 5 Hard) △

Enjoyment Level (1 Bad 5 Good) ♡

Overall Grade (1 Bad 5 Good) ☆

THE EXTRAS:

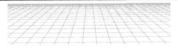

Notes
Facilities
Food & Water
Parking
Costs
Nature
Etc

∑ Personal Best Info
Hiking Totals etc

THE PLAN

Route Name

Visit No ☐

My Ref ☐

Meet up date / time/ location

Area Name

National Park ☐

Closest Town

GPS / Latitude & Longitude

Est. Duration

Grid Ref

Est. Distance

Km
Miles

Loop / Line & Back / One Way

Day Trip / Overnight / Holiday

Accommodation Info

Local Contact

THE EQUIPMENT

A   B

Camera Notes

Map Name / Ref

THE HIKE

Start Time

End Time

Actual Distance

(M) (P)

Total No of Steps

Calories
Burned

POINTS OF INTEREST

Difficulty Level (1 Easy 5 Hard) △

Enjoyment Level (1 Bad 5 Good) ♡

Overall Grade (1 Bad 5 Good) ☆

THE EXTRAS:

Notes
Facilities
Food & Water
Parking
Costs
Nature
Etc

∑ Personal Best Info
Hiking Totals etc

THE PLAN

Route Name

Visit No ☐
My Ref ☐

Meet up date / time/ location	Area Name National Park ☐
	Closest Town
Est. Duration	GPS / Latitude & Longitude
	Grid Ref
Est. Distance Km Miles	Loop / Line & Back / One Way Day Trip / Overnight / Holiday
	Accommodation Info
Local Contact	

THE EQUIPMENT

A   B

Camera Notes

Map Name / Ref

THE HIKE

Start Time

End Time

Actual Distance

Ⓜ Ⓟ

Total No of Steps

Calories Burned

POINTS OF INTEREST

Difficulty Level (1 Easy 5 Hard) △

Enjoyment Level (1 Bad 5 Good) ♡

Overall Grade (1 Bad 5 Good) ☆

THE EXTRAS:

Notes
Facilities
Food & Water
Parking
Costs
Nature
Etc

∑ Personal Best Info
Hiking Totals etc

THE PLAN

Route Name

Visit No ☐
My Ref ☐

Meet up date / time/ location

Area Name

National Park ☐

Closest Town

Est. Duration

GPS / Latitude & Longitude

Grid Ref

Est. Distance — Km / Miles

Loop / Line & Back / One Way   Day Trip / Overnight / Holiday

Local Contact

Accommodation Info

THE EQUIPMENT

A   B

Camera Notes

Map Name / Ref

THE HIKE

M   P

Start Time

End Time

Actual Distance

Total No of Steps   Calories Burned

POINTS OF INTEREST

Difficulty Level (1 Easy 5 Hard) △

Enjoyment Level (1 Bad 5 Good) ♡

Overall Grade (1 Bad 5 Good) ☆

THE EXTRAS:

Notes
Facilities
Food & Water
Parking
Costs
Nature
Etc

Personal Best Info
Hiking Totals etc

THE PLAN

Route Name

Visit No ☐

My Ref ☐

Meet up date / time/ location

Area Name   National Park ☐

Closest Town

GPS / Latitude & Longitude

Est. Duration

Grid Ref

Est. Distance   Km
                                 Miles

Loop / Line & Back / One Way   Day Trip / Overnight / Holiday

Accommodation Info

Local Contact

THE EQUIPMENT

A   B

Camera Notes   Map Name / Ref

THE HIKE

Start Time

End Time

Actual Distance

(M) (P)

Total No of Steps   Calories
                                     Burned

POINTS OF INTEREST

Difficulty Level (1 Easy 5 Hard) △

Enjoyment Level (1 Bad 5 Good) ♡

Overall Grade (1 Bad 5 Good) ☆

THE EXTRAS:

Notes
Facilities
Food & Water
Parking
Costs
Nature
Etc

Personal Best Info
Hiking Totals etc

THE PLAN

Route Name

Visit No ☐
My Ref ☐

Meet up date / time/ location

Area Name
National Park ☐

Closest Town

Est. Duration

GPS / Latitude & Longitude

Grid Ref

Est. Distance _____ Km / Miles

Loop / Line & Back / One Way   Day Trip / Overnight / Holiday

Accommodation Info

Local Contact

THE EQUIPMENT

A   B

Camera Notes

Map Name / Ref

THE HIKE

Start Time

End Time

Actual Distance

Total No of Steps

Calories Burned

(M) (P)

POINTS OF INTEREST

Difficulty Level (1 Easy 5 Hard)

Enjoyment Level (1 Bad 5 Good)

Overall Grade (1 Bad 5 Good)

THE EXTRAS:

Notes
Facilities
Food & Water
Parking
Costs
Nature
Etc

∑ Personal Best Info
Hiking Totals etc

THE PLAN

Route Name

Visit No ☐
My Ref ☐

Meet up date / time/ location

Area Name

National Park ☐

Closest Town

GPS / Latitude & Longitude

Est. Duration

Grid Ref

Est. Distance   Km / Miles

Loop / Line & Back / One Way   Day Trip / Overnight / Holiday

Accommodation Info

Local Contact

THE EQUIPMENT

A   B

Camera Notes

Map Name / Ref

THE HIKE

Start Time

End Time

Actual Distance

(M) (P)

Total No of Steps

Calories Burned

POINTS OF INTEREST

Difficulty Level (1 Easy 5 Hard) △

Enjoyment Level (1 Bad 5 Good) ♡

Overall Grade (1 Bad 5 Good) ☆

THE EXTRAS:

Notes
Facilities
Food & Water
Parking
Costs
Nature
Etc

Personal Best Info
Hiking Totals etc

THE PLAN

Route Name

Visit No ☐
My Ref ☐

Meet up date / time/ location

Area Name

National Park ☐

Closest Town

GPS / Latitude & Longitude

Est. Duration

Grid Ref

Est. Distance   Km
                       Miles

Loop / Line & Back / One Way   Day Trip / Overnight / Holiday

Local Contact

Accommodation Info

THE EQUIPMENT

A   B

Camera Notes

Map Name / Ref

THE HIKE

Start Time

End Time

Actual Distance

M   P

Total No of Steps

Calories
Burned

POINTS OF INTEREST

Difficulty Level (1 Easy 5 Hard) △

Enjoyment Level (1 Bad 5 Good) ♡

Overall Grade (1 Bad 5 Good) ☆

THE EXTRAS:

Notes
Facilities
Food & Water
Parking
Costs
Nature
Etc

∑ Personal Best Info
Hiking Totals etc

THE PLAN

Route Name

Visit No ☐
My Ref ☐

Meet up date / time/ location

Area Name

National Park ☐

Closest Town

GPS / Latitude & Longitude

Est. Duration

Grid Ref

Est. Distance   Km
Miles

Loop / Line & Back / One Way   Day Trip / Overnight / Holiday

Accommodation Info

Local Contact

THE EQUIPMENT

A   B

Camera Notes

Map Name / Ref

THE HIKE

Start Time

End Time

Actual Distance

Ⓜ   Ⓟ

Total No of Steps

Calories
Burned

POINTS OF INTEREST

Difficulty Level (1 Easy 5 Hard) △

Enjoyment Level (1 Bad 5 Good) ♡

Overall Grade (1 Bad 5 Good) ☆

THE EXTRAS:

Notes
Facilities
Food & Water
Parking
Costs
Nature
Etc

∑ Personal Best Info
Hiking Totals etc

THE PLAN

Route Name

Visit No ☐
My Ref ☐

Meet up date / time/ location

Area Name

National Park ☐

Closest Town

Est. Duration

GPS / Latitude & Longitude

Grid Ref

Est. Distance

Km
Miles

Loop / Line & Back / One Way   Day Trip / Overnight / Holiday

Accommodation Info

Local Contact

THE EQUIPMENT

A   B

Camera Notes

Map Name / Ref

THE HIKE

Start Time

End Time

Actual Distance

Ⓜ Ⓟ

Total No of Steps

Calories
Burned

POINTS OF INTEREST

Difficulty Level (1 Easy 5 Hard) △

Enjoyment Level (1 Bad 5 Good) ♡

Overall Grade (1 Bad 5 Good) ☆

THE EXTRAS:

Notes
Facilities
Food & Water
Parking
Costs
Nature
Etc

Personal Best Info
Hiking Totals etc

THE PLAN

Route Name

Visit No ☐
My Ref ☐

Meet up date / time/ location

Area Name   National Park ☐

Closest Town

GPS / Latitude & Longitude

Est. Duration

Grid Ref

Est. Distance   Km / Miles

Loop / Line & Back / One Way   Day Trip / Overnight / Holiday

Accommodation Info

Local Contact

THE EQUIPMENT

A   B

Camera Notes

Map Name / Ref

THE HIKE

Start Time

End Time

Actual Distance

(M)   (P)

Total No of Steps   Calories Burned

POINTS OF INTEREST

Difficulty Level (1 Easy 5 Hard) △

Enjoyment Level (1 Bad 5 Good) ♡

Overall Grade (1 Bad 5 Good) ☆

THE EXTRAS:

Notes
Facilities
Food & Water
Parking
Costs
Nature
Etc

Personal Best Info
Hiking Totals etc

THE PLAN

Route Name

Visit No ☐
My Ref ☐

Meet up date / time/ location

Area Name

National Park ☐

Closest Town

Est. Duration

GPS / Latitude & Longitude

Grid Ref

Est. Distance — Km / Miles

Loop / Line & Back / One Way

Day Trip / Overnight / Holiday

Local Contact

Accommodation Info

THE EQUIPMENT

A   B

Camera Notes

Map Name / Ref

THE HIKE

Start Time

End Time

Actual Distance

M   P

Total No of Steps

Calories Burned

POINTS OF INTEREST

Difficulty Level (1 Easy 5 Hard) △

Enjoyment Level (1 Bad 5 Good) ♡

Overall Grade (1 Bad 5 Good) ☆

THE EXTRAS:

Notes
Facilities
Food & Water
Parking
Costs
Nature
Etc

Personal Best Info
Hiking Totals etc

THE PLAN

Route Name

Visit No ☐
My Ref ☐

Meet up date / time/ location

Area Name   National Park ☐

Closest Town

GPS / Latitude & Longitude

Est. Duration

Grid Ref

Est. Distance   Km
                      Miles

Loop / Line & Back / One Way   Day Trip / Overnight / Holiday

Accommodation Info

Local Contact

THE EQUIPMENT

A   B

Camera Notes   Map Name / Ref

THE HIKE

Start Time

End Time

Actual Distance

(M) (P)

Total No of Steps   Calories
                                           Burned

POINTS OF INTEREST

Difficulty Level (1 Easy 5 Hard) △

Enjoyment Level (1 Bad 5 Good) ♡

Overall Grade (1 Bad 5 Good) ☆

THE EXTRAS:

Notes
Facilities
Food & Water
Parking
Costs
Nature
Etc

∑ Personal Best Info
  Hiking Totals etc

THE PLAN

Route Name

Visit No ☐
My Ref ☐

Meet up date / time/ location

Area Name

National Park ☐

Closest Town

GPS / Latitude & Longitude

Est. Duration

Grid Ref

Est. Distance   Km Miles

Loop / Line & Back / One Way   Day Trip / Overnight / Holiday

Accommodation Info

Local Contact

THE EQUIPMENT

A B

Camera Notes

Map Name / Ref

THE HIKE

M P

Start Time

End Time

Actual Distance

Total No of Steps   Calories Burned

POINTS OF INTEREST

Difficulty Level (1 Easy 5 Hard) △

Enjoyment Level (1 Bad 5 Good) ♡

Overall Grade (1 Bad 5 Good) ☆

THE EXTRAS:

Notes
Facilities
Food & Water
Parking
Costs
Nature
Etc

∑ Personal Best Info
  Hiking Totals etc

THE PLAN

Route Name

Visit No ☐
My Ref ☐

Meet up date / time/ location

Area Name   National Park ☐

Closest Town

GPS / Latitude & Longitude

Est. Duration

Grid Ref

Est. Distance   Km
                     Miles

Loop / Line & Back / One Way   Day Trip / Overnight / Holiday

Accommodation Info

Local Contact

THE EQUIPMENT

A   B

Camera Notes   Map Name / Ref

THE HIKE

Start Time

End Time

Actual Distance

(M) (P)

Total No of Steps   Calories
                                     Burned

POINTS OF INTEREST

Difficulty Level (1 Easy 5 Hard) △

Enjoyment Level (1 Bad 5 Good) ♡

Overall Grade (1 Bad 5 Good) ☆

THE EXTRAS:

Notes
Facilities
Food & Water
Parking
Costs
Nature
Etc

∑ Personal Best Info
  Hiking Totals etc

REVIEW NOTES

REVIEW NOTES

"After a day's walk, everything has twice its usual value." - G.M. Trevelyan

"When everything feels like an uphill struggle,
Just think of the view from the top." - Anonymous

Printed in Great Britain
by Amazon

34176343R00069